MAPS CHARTS GRAPHS

Neighborhoods   Level B

Sally J. Allen
Writer and Social Studies
Educational Consultant

Sharon M. Marosi
Project Editor

Remen-Willis Design Group
*Project Design and Illustration
and Cover Illustration*

Francyne Abate
Cover Design

Amy Van Hoose
Photo Research

Photographs: **2,** Chandoha Photography; **3,** A.J. Cunningham/Visuals Unlimited; **4a,** Ohio Department of Transportation; **4b,** NASA

ISBN 0-8136-2133-X

Printed in the United States of America

38 V011 15 14

1-800-321-3106
www.pearsonlearning.com

Pictures and Captions

WHAT I WILL LEARN   What can a picture show me?
How do **captions** help me?

Here is an **aerial photo.** It was made by taking a picture from an airplane.

CIRCLE IT

1. Circle the largest building in the picture.

2. Circle the bridge.

3. The bridge is _____ the largest building.

   above   **below**

4. Which is a water area?

   1   **2**   **3**

Look at these two pictures.

A

My Dragon by Chris Hert, Age 8

B

This raccoon is hungry.

The words below the pictures are called **captions.**
They help you learn more about the pictures.

CIRCLE IT

5. Which picture shows something drawn by a child?

   picture A   **picture B**

6. What animal is shown in picture A?

   dog   **dragon**   **horse**

7. What animal is in picture B?

   squirrel   **monkey**   **raccoon**

8. What is the animal in picture B doing?

   sleeping   **eating**   **running**

What Is a Map?

WHAT I WILL LEARN What is a **map**?
How is a map made?

Look at these three maps.

A

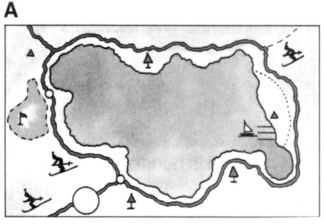

Pure Lake

B

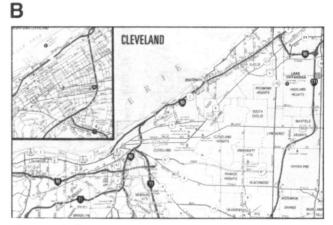

City of Cleveland

C

Satellite map of Earth

A map is a **model** of a real place. It shows a smaller picture of something that is too large to see all at once. Maps teach us about large places without our going there. Map A is a map of Pure Lake. Map B shows a large city.

Maps are made in several ways. Some maps are drawn after measuring the earth. Other maps are made by using facts about a certain place. Some maps are made from **aerial photos** of places on the earth. The newest maps are made by using satellites and computers. Map C on page 4 was made by a computer.

CIRCLE THE BEST ANSWER

1. Which map shows a city?

   map A   **map B**   **map C**

2. Which map shows Pure Lake?

   map A   **map B**   **map C**

3. A map is useful because it shows _____.

   a. **a lot in a small space**

   b. **things that don't change**

   c. **how something will look later**

4. Some maps are drawn by using _____.

   typewriters   **computers**   **telephones**

5. A map is a _____ of a real thing.

   model   **idea**   **book**

6. A map of our earth would be _____ than the earth.

   smaller   **larger**

7. What does map C show?

   Cleveland   **the earth**   **Pure Lake**

What Is a Globe?

WHAT I WILL LEARN What is a **globe**?
How is a globe different from a map?

Most maps are flat. They can be drawn on paper. A **globe** is a map that is not flat. It is round like a ball. A globe is a **model** of the earth. Here is a picture of a globe. It is not a real globe. A real globe would not fit in a flat book.

The globe on page 6 shows the half of the earth that we live on. This half is called the **Western Hemisphere.** That means the western half of the world.

Use the globe to help answer these questions.

CIRCLE IT

1. The girl is pointing to a water area on the globe. How is water shown on the globe?

   green color   **special lines**   **blue color**

2. How is land shown on this globe?

   special lines   **green and brown**   **dark words**

3. Circle the continent where you live on the globe.

4. Which does our hemisphere have more of?   **land**   **water**

MARK IT

5. Put an X on the Pacific Ocean on the globe.

6. Put a box ☐ on the Atlantic Ocean.

WRITE IT

Use a real globe in your schoolroom to find these answers.

7. What country is north of the United States?

   _____

8. In what ocean are the Hawaiian Islands?

   _____

Parts of a Map and Globe

WHAT I WILL LEARN
What are the parts of a map and a globe?

The parts of a map help you read it. Study the five parts
of this map.

A **title** tells you what a map shows. It helps you choose
the map you need.

A map **key** tells what the map **symbols** mean. The
symbols are the pictures or colors that stand for real
things on the map. A **compass** tells the four directions on
the map. It tells how the map matches the directions on
earth. North is toward the **North Pole.** South is toward
the **South Pole.** East is to the right of North. West is to
the left of North. **Labels** name special places on a map.
They may name streets, states, or cities.

WRITE IT

1. The title of this map is _____ .

MARK IT

2. Draw an *X* on the map key of this map.

3. <u>Underline</u> a label that names a street.

Globes usually have labels and a key. Often they do not have a title or compass.

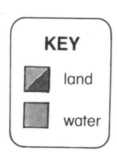

KEY

land

water

CIRCLE IT

4. What part of a map tells what symbols mean?

   title   **key**   **compass**

5. What part of a map shows directions on it?

   title   **key**   **compass**

6. A globe is a _____ of our earth.

   model   **picture**   **drawing**

7. Which one shows how the earth is shaped?   **map**   **globe**

Directions on a Map

WHAT I WILL LEARN   What are the four **cardinal directions?**
How do I find directions on a map?

Look at this map. The four **cardinal directions** are
shown on the **compass.** These directions are **north,
south, east,** and **west.**

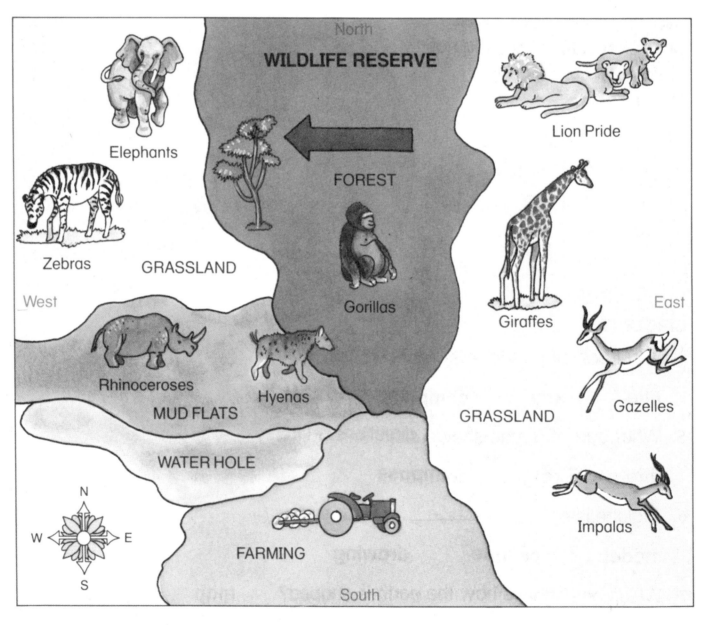

See how the compass shows directions in the same places as they are labeled on the map. Some maps have no direction labels. You can use the compass to label sides of a map.

Use this map to help answer these questions.

CIRCLE IT

1. In what area of the Wildlife Reserve is farming allowed?

   south   **west**   **north**   **east**

2. Gorillas are found _____ of the farming.

   south   **west**   **north**   **east**

3. What kind of area is in the east on this Reserve?

   grassland   **forest**   **water hole**

4. At night, the lion pride often follows the arrow shown on the map. In what direction do they move?

   north   **south**   **east**   **west**

5. In what direction do the elephants move to get water?

   north   **south**   **east**   **west**

6. What is west of the farming?

   hills   **forests**   **water hole**

WRITE IT

7. Finish this compass.
   Print all the directions.

South

A Grid

WHAT I WILL LEARN
How can I find a place on a **grid?**

Below is a grid called **Pioneer Trail.** To find a place on a grid, you must follow the numbers across the top, and the letters along the side of the grid. Use the grid to answer the questions on the next page.

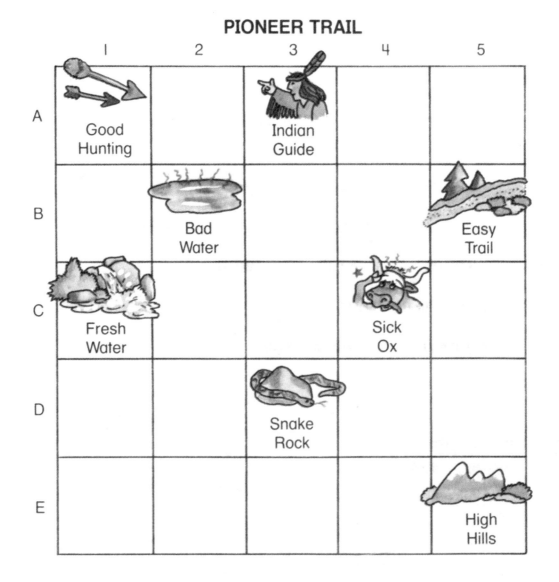

PIONEER TRAIL

CIRCLE IT

1. Go to row D. Find column 3. Find where the row and column meet. This location is called D-3. What is here?

   Fresh Water　　　**Indian Guide**　　　**Snake Rock**

2. Go to row A. Go over to column 5. What is this location called?

   A-1　　　**A-3**　　　**A-5**　　　**B-1**

3. What is at location C-4?

   Snake Rock　　　**Blank**　　　**Sick Ox**

4. What is the grid location of Bad Water?

   A-1　　　**B-2**　　　**C-1**　　　**B-4**

5. What is the grid location of High Hills?

   D-3　　　**D-4**　　　**E-1**　　　**E-5**

WRITE IT

Write what is found at these grid locations.

6. B-5

   _____

7. C-1

   _____

8. A-1

   _____

Signs and Symbols

WHAT I WILL LEARN
What do **signs** and **symbols** mean?

Signs and **symbols** are short picture messages. They tell us about things without using words.

Look at the signs on this page. They use symbols in place of words.

On this sign, the picture tells you what the sign means.

On the **No Smoking** sign, the red line across the cigarette is a symbol. It means **Do not smoke here.**

This sign shows a flame. That symbol means something catches fire easily.

Draw a line from each symbol to what it means.

MATCH IT

1.   Children cross here.

2.   Throw trash here.

3.   Danger! Rock may fall.

4.   Women's restroom.

5.   Do NOT drink or eat this.

Signs and symbols are used on maps. Symbols take the place of real things on a map. Here are some symbols often found on maps.

CIRCLE IT

Circle what each symbol means.

6.   city   farm   person

7.   school   church   store

8.   bridge   city   river

Map Symbols

WHAT I WILL LEARN
How do I use symbols on a map?

On the next page is a map of City Aquarium. Use the map symbols to help answer questions about the map. The **map key** gives the meaning of the symbols.

CIRCLE IT

1. Circle the symbol in the key that stands for Salt Water tanks.

2. Which one of these tanks has Fresh Water?

   4   1   5

3. Where are sea otters found? Find the number on the map.

   1   2   5

4. Which bench is closest to the Touch and Feel Table?
   Find its number on the map.

   4   9   8

DRAW IT

5. Put an X on the wall display that tells about Very Old Fish.

6. Put a box ☐ around the endangered species tank.

7. Draw a line from the Entrance to the Octopus and Squid Tank.

8. Draw a line from the Octopus and Squid Tank to the Exit.

CITY AQUARIUM

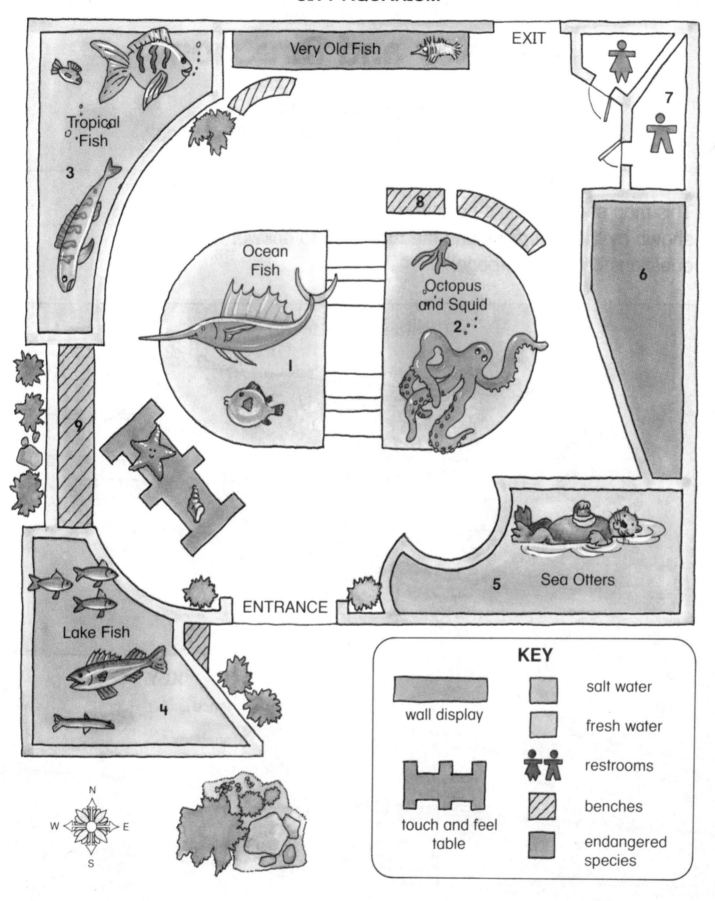

Very Old Fish

EXIT

Tropical Fish

3

Ocean Fish

1

8

Octopus and Squid

2

7

6

Sea Otters

5

ENTRANCE

Lake Fish

4

N
W   E
S

KEY

wall display	salt water
touch and feel table	fresh water
	restrooms
	benches
	endangered species

Map Key and Directions

WHAT I WILL LEARN
How can I find answers to problems with a map?

This map shows Chris's back yard. Use the directions shown by the **compass** and the **map key** to answer the questions on the next page.

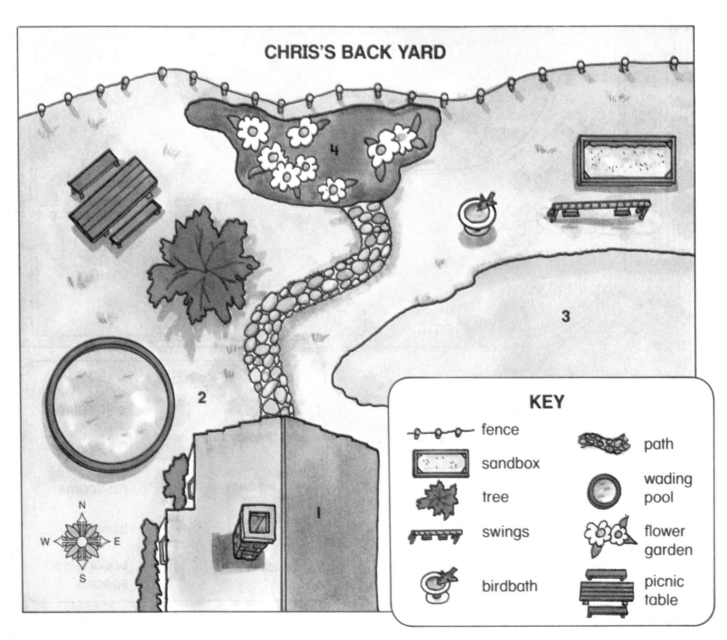

CHRIS'S BACK YARD

KEY

fence

sandbox

tree

swings

birdbath

path

wading pool

flower garden

picnic table

CIRCLE IT

1. Circle the birdbath in the key.

2. Where is the birdbath on the map?

   west of the swings   **west of the path**   **north of the sandbox**

3. Chris's mother wants to move the birdbath. She says the birds are frightened away by the children swinging and playing. The birds often sit on the fence north of the flower garden. Find the number from the map that shows the best new spot for the birdbath.

     I   3   4

4. Circle the tree on the map.

5. In what part of the yard is the garden found?

   north side   **west side**   **east side**

6. Chris's father wants to plant a new tree in the back yard. It should be away from other trees. It should have a lot of empty space around it. Which spot would be best for the new tree?

     I   2   3

7. Where is the children's wading pool?

   a. **east of the flower garden**

   b. **north of the path**

   c. **south of the picnic table**

8. Where should a box of water toys be kept in the back yard?

     I   2   3

Map Scale and Distance

WHAT I WILL LEARN What is **scale** on a map?
How does scale show distance on a map?

Think of trying to draw a map of your back yard. Your back yard is much larger than a piece of paper. You would have to make distances shorter on paper. A large object would have to be drawn smaller on the paper.

On a map, a short distance, like I inch ├────────┤, stands for a long distance, like 10 feet. **Scale** shows what small distance stands for a larger, real distance.

Shelly drew a map of her vegetable garden. First, she measured the garden. It was 4 feet long and 4 feet wide. She decided to let I inch stand for I foot on her map. She marked off four I-inch marks in a line like this.

| 0 | I | 2 | 3 | 4 |

This shows how long Shelly's garden would be on her map.

The next page shows how Shelly drew her garden on a piece of paper.

Look at the scale on the map of Shelly's garden.
One inch on the map shows one foot of real-life distance
in Shelly's garden.

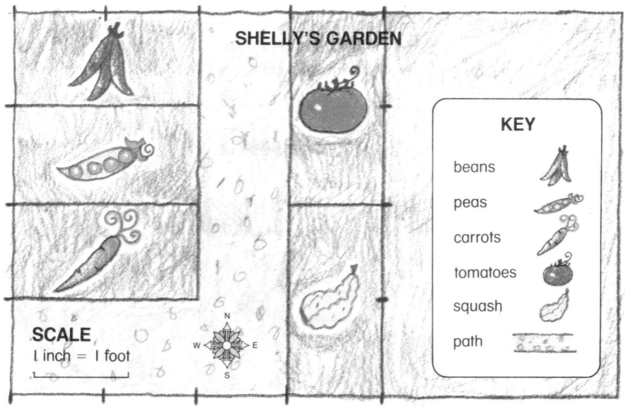

SHELLY'S GARDEN

SCALE
1 inch = 1 foot

KEY

beans

peas

carrots

tomatoes

squash

path

CIRCLE IT

1. The areas for beans, peas, and carrots are all 2 inches
   wide on the map. How wide are they in real life?

   2 inches   2 feet   1 foot

2. Shelly walked from the north end of her garden to the
   south end along the path. How many feet did she
   walk?

   4 feet   2 feet   1 foot

3. How wide are the tomato and squash areas on the map?

   3 inches   2 feet   1 inch

4. How wide are the tomato and squash areas in real life?

   3 feet   2 inches   1 foot

Using Map Scale

WHAT I WILL LEARN
How do I read the **scale** on a map?

Use the map and its scale to answer the questions on the next page.

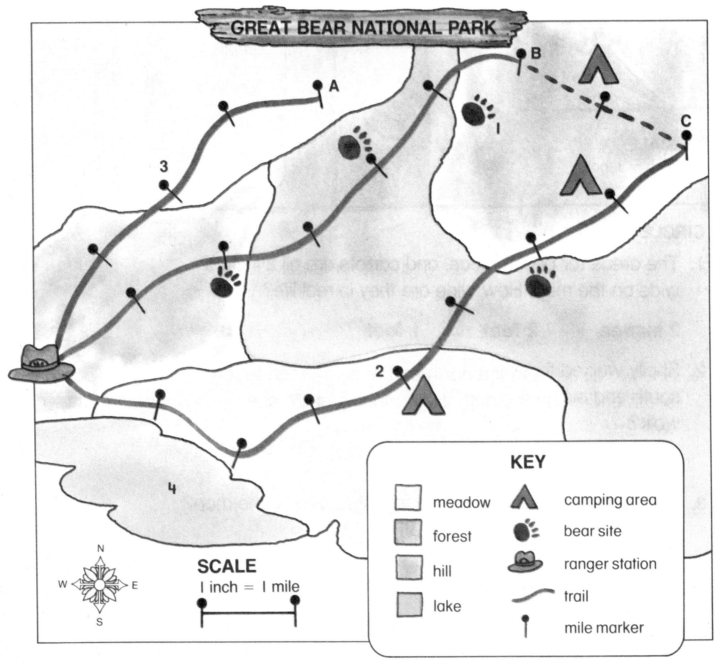

GREAT BEAR NATIONAL PARK

KEY

meadow   camping area

forest   bear site

hill   ranger station

lake   trail

   mile marker

SCALE
1 inch = 1 mile

N W E S

CIRCLE IT

1. How many miles are shown by 1 inch on this map?

   5   1   2

2. What is the real distance of the shortest trail in the park?

   4 miles   1 inch   6 miles

3. What is the real distance of the longest park trail?

   4 miles   6 miles   8 miles

4. What trail goes by the most bear sites?

   A   B   C

5. How far is it from the ranger station to the nearest bear site in the park?

   2 miles   4 miles   1 mile

6. How far is the nearest camping area from the ranger station?

   2 miles   4 miles   5 miles

7. If the park wanted to connect trails B and C along the dotted line, how many more miles would need to be built?

   1 mile   2 miles   3 miles

8. A new camping area will be built. Which number on the map shows the best place for it?

   1   3   4

Using a Road Map

WHAT I WILL LEARN   How do I compare distances on a road map?
How do I read information and find directions on a **road map?**

On the next page is a **road map.** Sometimes we call this
a **highway map.** It is useful for finding the best way to
get somewhere. Use the map to answer these questions.
You will be using the scale and direction.

CIRCLE IT

1. What highway connects Rock Corners and Red Bluff?

   (85)   (7)   (75)

2. What city lies on the road between Red Bluff and
   Freeburg?

   Maple Grove   **Oak Town**   **Rock Corners**

3. What is the first city east of Maple Grove?

   Rock Corners   **Oak Town**   **Pleasantville**

4. In what direction does a person travel to get from
   Freeburg to Red Bluff?

   east   **south**   **north**   **west**

5. How many miles is it from Old Mill to Elmville?   1   **2**   **3**

6. Which one of the three routes shown on the map is the
   longest?

   yellow   **purple**   **green**

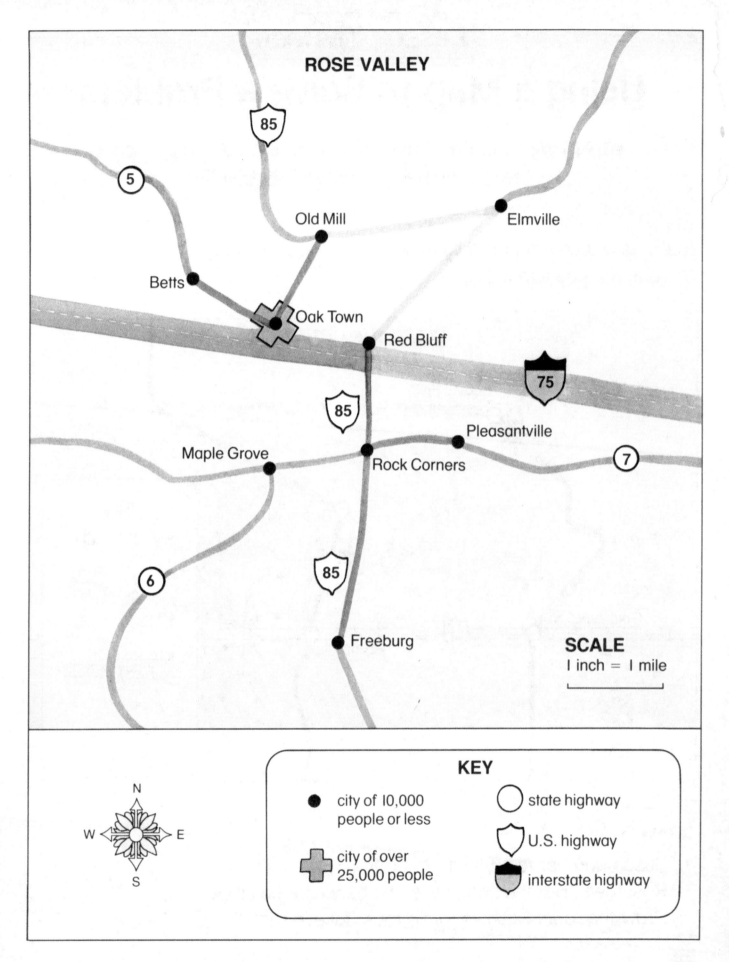

ROSE VALLEY

Old Mill

Elmville

Betts

Oak Town

Red Bluff

Maple Grove

Rock Corners

Pleasantville

Freeburg

SCALE

1 inch = 1 mile

KEY

● city of 10,000 people or less

✚ city of over 25,000 people

◯ state highway

⬠ U.S. highway

🛡 interstate highway

Using a Map to Solve a Problem

WHAT I WILL LEARN   How can a map help solve a problem?
Can a map help me answer questions?

Below is a road map of Chipmunk County. Use the map
to solve the problem below.

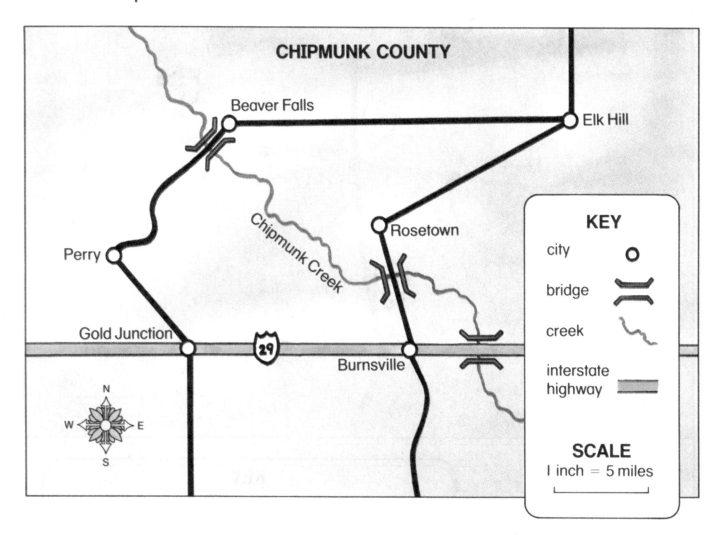

DRAW IT

1. Susan and her family want to go from Burnsville to
   Rosetown. But the bridge is down between the cities.
   Draw the route Susan's family must take in red.

Use the map of Marysville to answer the questions below.

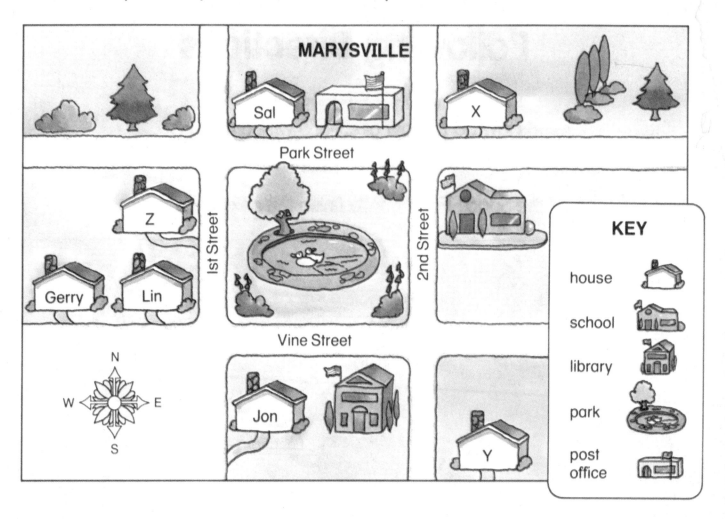

CIRCLE IT

2. What street is the library on?

   I st   Park   Vine

3. What corner is the school on?

   2nd and Park   **I st and Vine**   **I st and Park**

4. Whose house is north of the park?

   Lin's   **Sal's**   **Jon's**   **Gerry's**

5. Lin's family wants to move closer to the school.
   What house would be best for them?

   X house   **Y house**   **Z house**

Lesson Fourteen

Following Directions

WHAT I WILL LEARN
How do I follow directions with a map?

Use the map of the Space Fun Park to finish the next page.

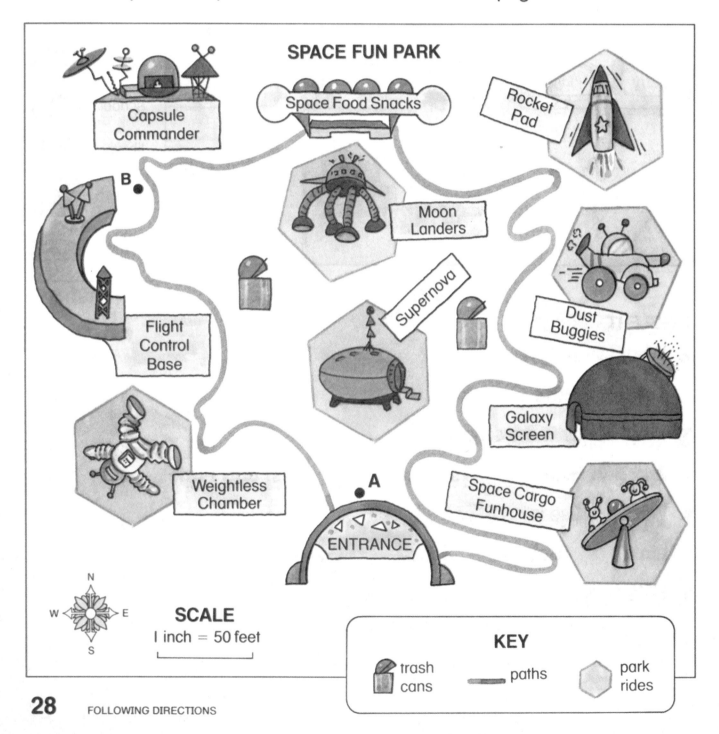

SPACE FUN PARK

Capsule Commander

Space Food Snacks

Rocket Pad

B

Moon Landers

Supernova

Dust Buggies

Flight Control Base

Galaxy Screen

Weightless Chamber

A

Space Cargo Funhouse

ENTRANCE

N W E S

SCALE
I inch = 50 feet

KEY
trash cans
paths
park rides

MARK IT

1. Put an **X** on the ride north of the Dust Buggies.

2. Put a ☐ around the ride east of the Entrance.

3. Draw a triangle △ around the area west of the Space Food Snacks.

WRITE IT

4. Tom walked in a straight line from Point A to Point B.

   Tom walked _____ feet.

5. What does this symbol stand for on the map?

   _____

TRACE IT

6. Han went first to the Supernova. Then, he went to the Flight Control Base. Next, he went straight north to a ride. Finally, he headed for the Snack Bar to meet his dad. Draw his route in **blue** on the map.

7. Peg went first to the Space Cargo Funhouse. Then, she went north to the next area. Next, she went to the Moon Landers. Finally, she went to Capsule Commander. Draw her route in **red** on the map. Use arrows to show the direction she went.

Finding Real Places Far Away

WHAT I WILL LEARN
Where are important places in our world?

Here is a map of the earth.

THE EARTH

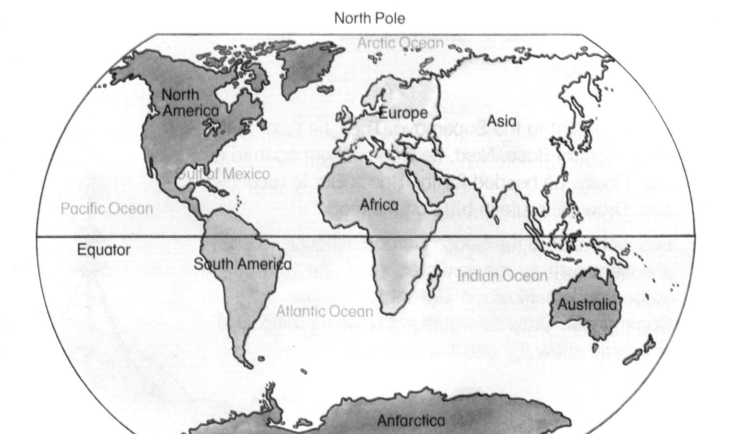

Use the map of the earth to answer these questions.

A **continent** is a very large body of land. The continents are named in large black letters. An **ocean** is a very large body of water. The oceans and other bodies of water are named in blue print.

CIRCLE IT

1. Circle the name **Equator** on the map.

2. The Equator divides our world into _____.

   a north part and a south part
   an east part and a west part

3. Which continent is the Gulf of Mexico nearest?

   Asia   **Africa**   **North America**

4. Which ocean is the farthest north?

   Pacific Ocean   **Indian Ocean**   **Arctic Ocean**

5. Which one of these continents is south of Asia?

   North America   **Europe**   **Australia**

6. Which continent is the largest?

   North America   **Europe**   **Asia**

7. Circle **Africa** on the map.

WRITE IT

8. Name two continents that touch the Equator.

   _____

   _____

Finding Real Places Near Me

WHAT I WILL LEARN   Where is my state located?
Where are important places in the United States? Where are
major cities found in the United States?

Use the map of the United States to finish this page.

CIRCLE IT

1. Circle this place in red.   **Gulf of Mexico**

2. Circle this place in blue.   **Mississippi River**

3. Circle this place in yellow.   **Washington, D.C.**

4. Circle this state in brown.   **Alaska**

COLOR IT

5. Color your state green.

WRITE IT

Look up answers in an atlas if you need to.

6. Write the name of your state's capital city.

_____

7. Write the name of the capital city of the United States.

_____

8. Write the name of one mountain chain in the United States.

_____

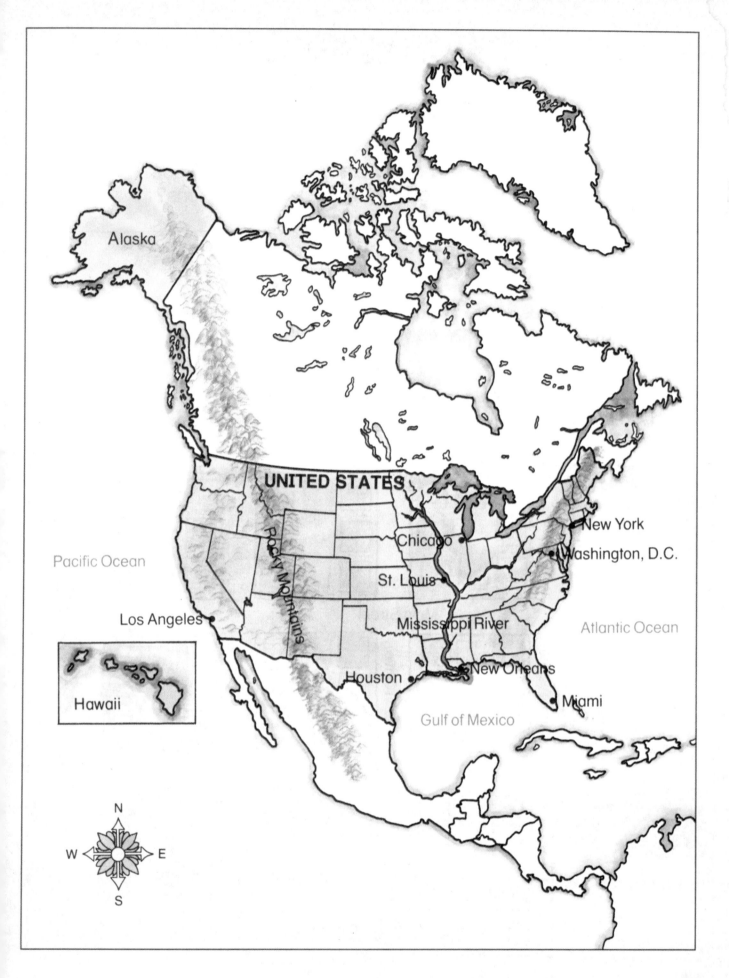

Alaska

UNITED STATES

Pacific Ocean

New York

Washington, D.C.

Chicago

St. Louis

Rocky Mountains

Los Angeles

Hawaii

Mississippi River

Atlantic Ocean

Houston

New Orleans

Miami

Gulf of Mexico

N

W · E

S

Special Maps

WHAT I WILL LEARN Why are **special maps** made?
How do I use a special map to answer questions?

Special maps are made to show just one thing.

This special map was made for just one purpose. The purpose
is to show where blue star homes are in Kate's neighborhood.

BLUE STAR HOMES

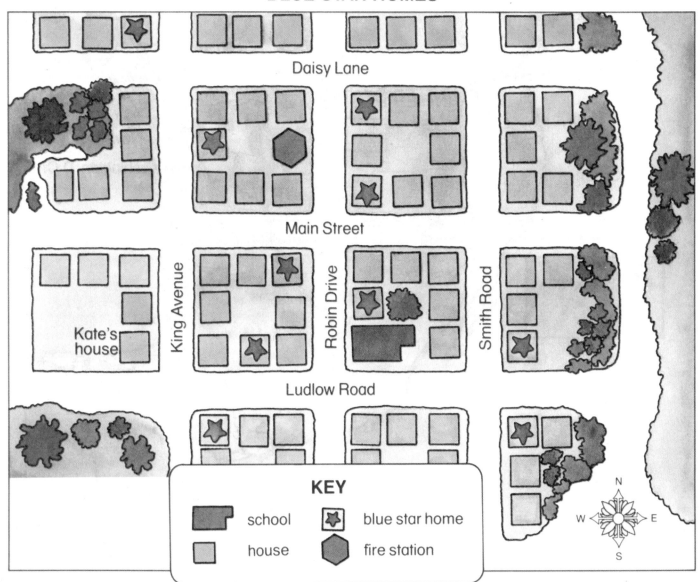

Many neighborhoods have blue star homes. These homes are safe places for kids who need help on their way to or from school. If a big dog frightened you, you could stop at a blue star home and ask for help.

Now use the map of blue star homes in Kate's neighborhood to answer these questions.

DRAW IT

1. Draw a box ☐ around the blue star home closest to the school.

2. Draw a circle around the blue star home that is east of the school.

3. Draw a straight line north from the school as far as you can go.

4. Circle any blue star homes on your line north of the school.

CIRCLE IT

5. How many blue star homes are shown on this map?

   5   7   10

6. If Kate walks straight west of the school on her way home, how many blue star homes does she pass?

   1   2   3

7. Why is a special map made?

   a. to show many things

   b. to show many places

   c. to show just one thing

Pictographs

WHAT I WILL LEARN What does a **pictograph** tell me? How do I read a pictograph?

Here is a pictograph. It uses pictures to show how many different kinds of transportation students saw on a class trip.

The words at the bottom of the pictograph tell what kinds of transportation the students saw.

The numbers along the left side of the pictograph tell how many of each kind of transportation the students saw.

KINDS OF TRANSPORTATION

	Buses	Cars	Trucks	Trains	Airplanes
10					
9			🚚		
8		🚗	🚚		
7		🚗	🚚		
6		🚗	🚚		
5		🚗	🚚		✈️
4		🚗	🚚		✈️
3	🚌	🚗	🚚	🚂	✈️
2	🚌	🚗	🚚	🚂	✈️
1	🚌	🚗	🚚	🚂	✈️

In some pictographs, you count from the left to the right.
In this pictograph, you count from the bottom to the top.
Use the pictograph on page 36 to answer these questions.

CIRCLE IT

1. What does the pictograph show?

   kinds of cars   kinds of transportation   vacations

2. How many different kinds of transportation are shown?

   5   28   9

3. How many buses did the class see?

   I   3   5

4. How many cars did the class see?

   3   5   8

5. What kind of transportation did the class see most often?

   cars   trucks   airplanes

6. The class saw the same number of what two kinds of transportation?

   cars and trucks   buses and trains   trucks and trains

7. The class saw _____ airplanes.

   3   5   6

WRITE IT

8. Write the name of another kind of transportation that the class may have seen.

   _____

Making a Tallygram

WHAT I WILL LEARN Why is a **tallygram** made?
How do I read a tallygram?

The students in Mr. Job's class live in four different kinds of homes. They made a **tallygram** to show how many students live in each kind of home. To **tally** means to **count.** A tallygram makes counting things easier because you count by fives.

This tallygram shows how many students in Mr. Job's class live in apartments and in townhouses.

HOMES IN OUR NEIGHBORHOOD		
Apartments		卌 I
Townhouses		IIII
Houses		
Duplexes		

See how Mr. Job made the tallygram.

Six of Mr. Job's students live in apartments. First, Mr. Job put four marks beside **apartments.**

Apartments		IIII

Then he made a fifth mark across the other four marks to show **5**.

There was only one more apartment, so he made one more mark to show **6**.

MARK IT

1. There were 10 houses and 8 duplexes counted by the class. Tally those on the tallygram.

CIRCLE IT

2. Which kind of home had the lowest tally?

   apartments   **houses**   **townhouses**

3. Which kind of home had the highest tally?

   apartments   **houses**   **duplexes**

MARK IT

4. Complete the tallygram below. It tells how Mr. Job's students get to school. Use these numbers:

   7 children walk to school
   8 children ride the bus
   6 children come by car

HOW MR. JOB'S CLASS COME TO SCHOOL	
	Number of students
Walk	ℍℍ ||
Bus	
Car	

Using Bar Graphs

WHAT I WILL LEARN   How do I read a **bar graph?**
Can I compare facts on a bar graph?

A **bar graph** is made by using bars to show how much or
how many. Gil made this bar graph after he made a
tallygram. Gil asked people in his neighborhood what they do
to keep it clean. He marked their answers on a
tallygram. Then he used the tallygram to make this graph.

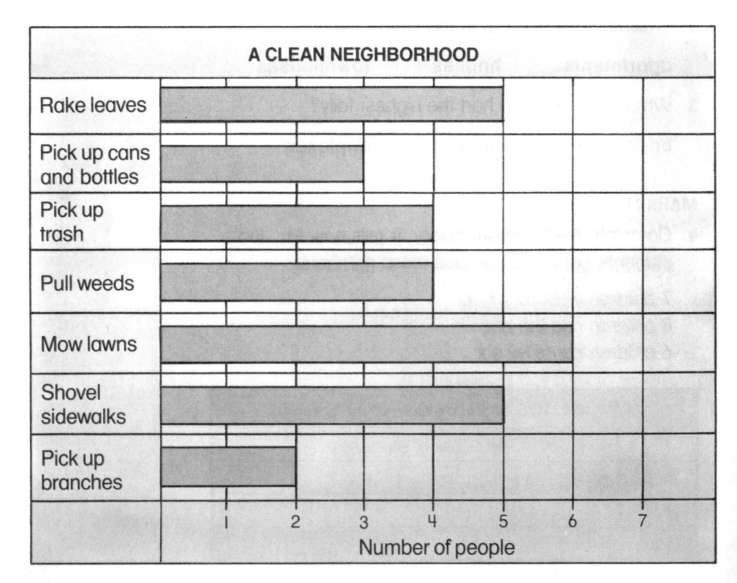

A CLEAN NEIGHBORHOOD

Use the bar graph on page 40 to answer these questions.

CIRCLE IT

1. What does Gil's bar graph show?

   a. Gil's jobs

   b. jobs done on a farm

   c. how a neighborhood is kept clean

2. How many people pull weeds?

   4   5   6

3. How many people pick up trash?

   2   3   4

4. What job do six people do?

   pick up trash   mow lawns   shovel sidewalks

5. How many people rake leaves?

   3   4   5

6. How many more people shovel sidewalks than pick up bottles and cans?

   1   2   3

7. What job do the fewest people do?

   a. mow lawns

   b. shovel sidewalks

   c. pick up branches

Using Charts

WHAT I WILL LEARN   What is a **chart?**
How do I read charts?

A **chart** is a picture that shows how something happens.

FROM TREES TO PRODUCTS

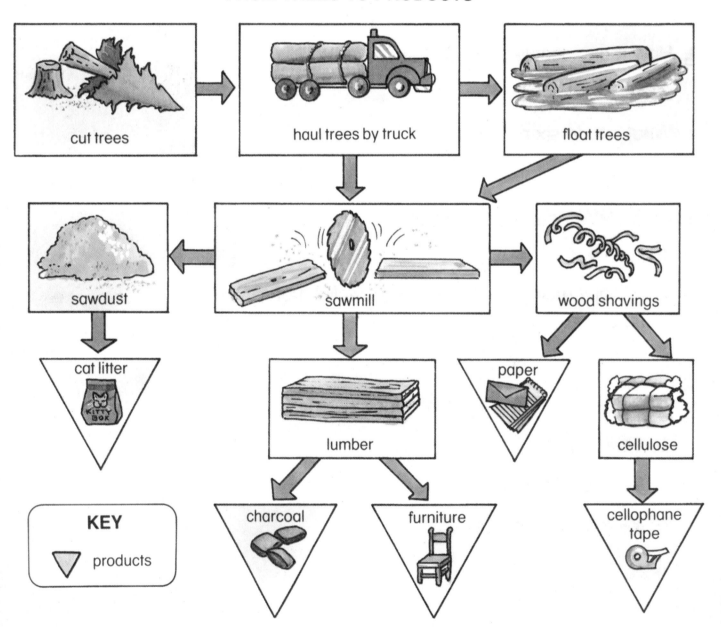

cut trees

haul trees by truck

float trees

sawdust

sawmill

wood shavings

cat litter

lumber

paper

cellulose

KEY

products

charcoal

furniture

cellophane tape

Use the chart on page 42 to answer these questions.
Follow the arrows on the chart to see how trees in a
forest become products we use.

CIRCLE IT

1. What happens right after the trees are cut?

2. Circle three things that come straight from the sawmill.

   wood shavings   **paper**   **lumber**

   sawdust   **cellulose**   **furniture**

3. What is made from sawdust?

   furniture   **cellophane tape**   **cat litter**

4. How do trees get to the sawmill?

   by water only   **by water or truck**   **by truck only**

5. What does this chart show you?

   a. **how trees become products**

   b. **how trees are cut**

   c. **how cellophane tape is made**

6. What two products are made from lumber?

   paper and   **charcoal and**   **paper and**
   cat litter   **furniture**   **cellophane tape**

7. Use the key to count the number of products
   shown on the chart.

   There are _____ products.

   5   **7**   **3**

Aerial Photograph a picture taken from an airplane or helicopter

Atlas a book of maps

Bar Graph graph that uses bar shapes to compare how much

Caption words below a picture that tell what the picture is about

Cardinal Directions the four directions, north, south, east and west

Chart a picture that shows how something happens

Compass the symbol on a map that shows the four cardinal directions

Continent a very large body of land

Equator an imaginary line that divides the Earth into a north part and a south part

Globe a round model of the Earth

Grid lines that form rows and columns to locate points easily

Highway Map a road map

Map a drawing of a place that uses pictures to stand for real things

Map Key a list of symbols on a map, and what they mean

Map Scale a small distance that stands for a larger, real distance

Ocean a very large body of water

Pictograph a graph that uses pictures to tell how many

Sign a short picture message

Special Map a map made to show just one thing

Symbol a picture that stands for a real thing

Tallygram a graph that shows how many by counting by fives

Title a name that tells what a map or picture is about

Western Hemisphere the half of the Earth that we live in

Answer Key

Lesson One

1. (largest building circled)
2. (bridge circled)
3. above
4. 2
5. picture A
6. dragon
7. raccoon
8. eating

Lesson Two

1. map B
2. map A
3. a. a lot in a small space
4. computers
5. model
6. smaller
7. the earth

Lesson Three

1. blue color
2. green and brown
3. (North America circled)
4. water
5. (an X on the Pacific Ocean)
6. (a box on the Atlantic Ocean)
7. Canada
8. Pacific Ocean

Lesson Four

1. Pete's Neighborhood
2. (an X on the map key)
3. (one street name underlined)
4. key
5. compass
6. model
7. globe

Lesson Five

1. south
2. north
3. grassland
4. west
5. south
6. water hole

7.

Lesson Six

1. Snake Rock
2. A-5
3. Sick Ox
4. B-2
5. E-5
6. Easy Trail
7. Fresh Water
8. Good Hunting

Lesson Seven

1-5.

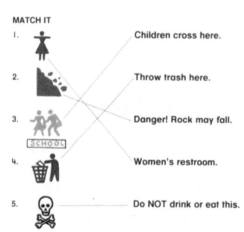

6. city
7. church
8. river

Lesson Eight

I, 5-8.

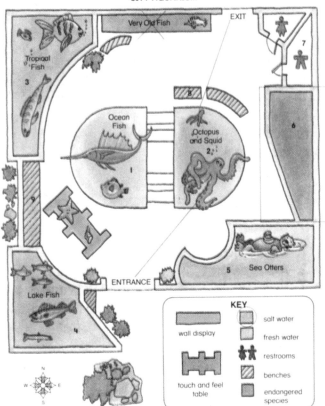

CITY AQUARIUM

2. 4
3. 5
4. 9

Lesson Nine

1. (birdbath in key circled)
2. west of the swings
3. 4
4. (tree on map circled)
5. north side
6. 3
7. c. south of the picnic table
8. 2

Lesson Ten

1. 2 feet
2. 4 feet
3. I inch
4. I foot

Lesson Eleven

1. I
2. 4 miles
3. 8 miles
4. B
5. 2 miles
6. 4 miles
7. 2 miles
8. 3

Lesson Twelve

1. 85
2. Rock Corners
3. Rock Corners
4. north
5. 2
6. yellow

Lesson Thirteen

1.

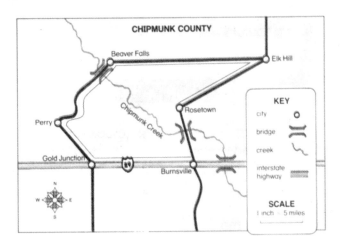

CHIPMUNK COUNTY

2. Vine
3. 2nd and Park
4. Sal's
5. X house

1-3,6,7.

4. 200
5. trash cans

Lesson Fifteen

1. (Equator circled)
2. a north part and a south part
3. North America
4. Arctic Ocean
5. Australia
6. Asia

7. (Africa circled)
8. South America
   Africa

Lesson Sixteen

1. (Gulf of Mexico circled in red)
2. (Mississippi River circled in blue)
3. (Washington D.C. circled in yellow)
4. (Alaska circled in brown)

5,6. Answers will vary.
7. Washington, D.C.
8. Rocky or Appalachian Mountains, for example

Lesson Seventeen

1-4.

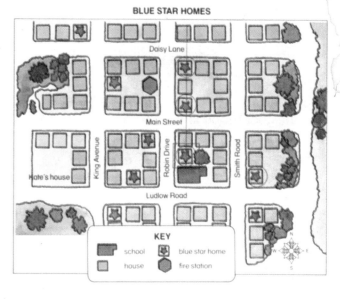

5. 10
6. 2

7. c. to show just one thing

Lesson Eighteen

1. kinds of transportation
2. 5
3. 3
4. 8

5. trucks
6. buses and trains
7. 5
8. Answers may vary.

Lesson Nineteen

1.

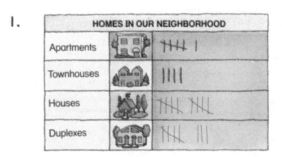

HOMES IN OUR NEIGHBORHOOD

Apartments		卌 l
Townhouses		llll
Houses		卌 卌
Duplexes		卌 lll

2. townhouses
3. houses

HOW MR. JOB'S CLASS COME TO SCHOOL	
	Number of students
Walk	┼┼┼┼ II
Bus	THL III
Car	THL I

Lesson Twenty

1. c. how a
   neighborhood is
   kept clean
2. 4
3. 4

4. mow lawns
5. 5
6. 2
7. c. pick up
   branches

1.
2. wood shavings
   sawdust
   lumber
3. cat litter

4. by water or truck
5. a. how trees
   become products
6. charcoal and
   furniture
7. 5